Celebrate you!

BUILDING YOUR SELF-ESTEEM

▲▲▲▲▲▲▲▲▲▲▲▲▲▲▲▲▲▲▲▲▲▲▲▲▲▲▲▲▲

BUILDING YOUR SELF-ESTEEM

▲▲▲▲▲▲▲▲▲▲▲▲▲▲▲▲▲▲▲▲▲▲▲▲▲▲▲▲▲▲

JULIE TALLARD JOHNSON

WITH AN INTRODUCTION BY PAMELA KENNEDY, JR., AGE 18

LERNER PUBLICATIONS COMPANY ▲ MINNEAPOLIS

LIBRARY OF CONGRESS CATALOGING-IN-PUBLICATION DATA

Johnson, Julie Tallard
    Celebrate you! : building your self-esteem / Julie Tallard Johnson:
with an introduction by Pamela Kennedy.
        p.   cm.
    Includes bibliographical references and index.
    Summary: Describes the fundamentals of self-esteem and ways to
boost self-esteem.
    ISBN 0-8225-0046-9
    1. Self-respect—Juvenile literature. [1. Self-respect.]
I. Title.
BF697.5 S46J64   1991
158'.1—dc20   90-38876
                                                      CIP
                                                      AC

Manufactured in the United States of America

    2   3   4   5   6   7   8   9   10   00   99   98   97   96   95   94   93   92

Acknowledgments

First I want to acknowledge the many young adults whose wisdom and honesty made this book a reality. Their names and stories fill each page of the book. And more specifically, thanks to Anna Swanson, Pamela Kennedy, Jr., Marnie Johnson, Keri Simonson, Eric Taylor, and Jennifer Holland.

I am grateful to Paul Hildebrandt, Ph.D., for providing a background of knowledge and support for this book.

I am grateful for LeeAnne Engfer, whose editing talents improved upon every page of this book.

Others who added support and insight in their special ways include Kristine Merrill, Vicky Fry, Doug Swanson, my mother Barb, and everyone in the Monday night Course in Miracles class.

Finally, I am grateful to my teenage friendships whose memory and presence are forever a part of my celebration of life.

This book is lovingly dedicated to Cayce, Shelby, Elliot, Cecilia, Spencer, Lyndsay, Cody, and Haley.

CONTENTS

Somewhere

I've lost a piece of me
   somewhere,
and I've looked everywhere.
I've looked at old pictures, I've held your hand and swung
over cracks in the sidewalk,
   but somewhere lies a piece of me.

It isn't just the piece that left when you died,
It isn't in the regrets and reprimands that shower my life,
   maybe it's a piece I never had.

I hold images of mom in her handkerchief—
pitching a softball, of cornfields and thunderstorms, of
violets and daisy chains, of life and death.

But somewhere in the smell of damp Illinois dirt, in the
clover, in the alcoholic turmoil, I lost a piece of me.

And now that I'm putting a life together,
   I want it back.

INTRODUCTION

When I attempt to visualize my "missing piece," I only
see something intangible and still at times unknown to me.
I know it includes a link to a healthy attitude about myself;
in it is the power to understand myself as I truly am—
unclouded by low self-esteem. This piece is the catalyst
that will allow me to become the person I want to become.

I often expect to see this giant "something" out of the
corner of my eye and discover the missing piece of myself.
But I realize that this missing piece isn't some solid mass to
be picked up and carried away. It comes in small experiences, feelings, and changed attitudes about myself and my
world, such as the time I finally finished a term paper.
When I completed the paper I felt the missing piece shrink
a little and something good grow in its place. When people
I trust compliment me, the good in me multiplies again. I

know I have to believe in myself, in my abilities, and in my capacity for love and for learning—and for the adult life that is approaching.

For you the missing piece may be your self-esteem, or it may be something less definable. But if you believe in yourself, using the techniques discussed in this book, you will discover that everyone is worthy of love and respect—and this includes you. In fact, I have come to realize that it is essential to love and respect myself.

I still look for my missing piece in the situations that have gone by and in my family relationships. But I can only hold on to someone else's hand for so long; eventually there are cracks in the sidewalk that even your parents can't carry you over. I have learned a lot about treating myself in healthy and loving ways from this book. I have also learned to trust others and let them support my dreams.

The missing piece is shrinking and I am ready to celebrate my years as an adult.

Pamela Kennedy, Jr.
age 18

CHAPTER ONE

What Is Self-Esteem?

*What lies behind us and what lies before us
are tiny matters compared to what lies
within us.*

—Ralph Waldo Emerson

When I began to write this book, I told one of my teenage friends, Anna, about it. She smiled and said, "Oh, *self-esteem,* we teenagers don't have any." It is true that many young adults lack self-esteem. Your teen years can, however, be the most important time for building your self-esteem. You have the power to make great things happen for you right now, if you choose. That power is what self-esteem is all about.

The teenage years are full of changes, as you know. Your body is in constant flux, your emotions tend to be very intense, and you seem to fall somewhere between childhood and adulthood. This is an excellent time to focus on yourself and your self-esteem. Who you are now will say a lot about what kind of an adult you will become.

Besides the basic necessities of water, food, shelter, and

clothing, we each need love and acceptance—we need to feel good about ourselves. Each of us needs self-esteem. Everyone has problems and struggles, but without self-esteem, life is more painful and difficult. Many things are outside of our control—such as our age, the weather, who our parents are, and other people's behavior. But there are many things within our control: how we think and feel and how we respond to the world around us. Self-esteem includes our beliefs, thoughts, feelings, and desires; self-esteem is what we have *within* us.

Your Self-Esteem:

beliefs   **wishes**

thoughts   **desires**   **feelings**

attitudes   **wants**

We all want to love and be loved, to be accepted, and to be admired. Many of us do a lot of harmful things in an attempt to feel good: we take drugs, lie or cheat, eat too much junk food, act dangerously to show off. But none of these behaviors gives us a lasting sense of feeling good. In fact, they usually make us feel worse about ourselves. Self-esteem is about achieving a lasting experience of feeling good about ourselves.

Positive self-esteem is rooted in a deep acceptance of yourself, despite your shortcomings, mistakes, or disabilities. It includes accepting responsibility for your own well-being and taking full charge of your life. Your primary responsibility in life is your own development and well-being.

Growing into adulthood means becoming responsible for the consequences of your choices and behaviors. Regardless of outside circumstances, such as rude teachers, a physical disability, peer pressure, divorced parents, or even abusive parents, you can build your self-esteem. *You have the power to feel good about yourself.*

The Still-Famous Marilyn Monroe

You probably know about Marilyn Monroe. She was a talented actress. On the outside she had everything—beauty, wealth, and fame. On the inside she was very unhappy. She didn't really like herself. No matter how popular she became, how many movies she starred in, or how many men she dated, she was still unhappy. Marilyn's father abandoned her when she was young, and her mother was in and out of mental institutions all her life. Perhaps no one taught Marilyn about self-esteem—that the lasting sense of feeling good can only come from within us. At the age of 36, she killed herself.

Attractive, talented people—even famous people like Marilyn Monroe—are not guaranteed self-esteem. Smart kids don't necessarily feel good about themselves, and athletes are just as likely to feel lonely and depressed as people who are not athletic. Self-esteem means feeling good about ourselves, what we do, and our relationships, regardless of what's going on around us. Self-esteem is *not* an evaluation of how good a person we are, however, or how much we accomplish.

Furthermore, self-esteem is not something you either have or don't have. Everyone varies in how good they feel about themselves. Some of us feel really great about one area of our life, such as musical skill, while we lack esteem in other areas, such as personal relationships. Self-esteem is something you can increase.

Beth Isn't Perfect

Beth may sound familiar to you. Beth is 16 years old and has just moved to a new school. She is a good athlete and usually makes the swim team or competes in some sport. Many students consider her popular and attractive. Beth does well in most of her classes, and the teachers find her easy to get along with. But it seems that no matter what Beth does, she never quite feels good about herself. In fact, she doesn't tell many people this, but most of the time she feels embarrassed—embarrassed about when she does well *and* embarrassed about her mistakes. On the surface, she is bright, easygoing, and accomplished in school. On the inside, she is angry, depressed, and unsure of herself. How can this be?

Beth believes she has to do everything perfectly. She is often disappointed with herself because she finds something wrong with whatever she does. She always thinks she could do better. If she gets three As, one B, and a C, the C is her proof that she is a failure. When she makes a mistake during the day, it is the mistake that gets her attention. Beth is never completely happy with herself, because she always falls short of perfection.

Perfectionism is the strong belief that you have to do things right, or perfectly. This belief is one of the most common threats to self-esteem. If you are a perfectionist, you often feel that you have "missed the mark" or need to do better. You often put things off because you're afraid you won't do them "right." You might begin projects but not complete them. You may take on too many projects or classes at school and have little or no time left for fun. Because you're so concerned about doing things right, you either put things off or never feel good about your accomplishments. Perfectionism blocks your ability to enjoy your teenage years and celebrate your accomplishments.

Many teens feel unable to keep up with others in school or extracurricular activities. They see themselves as "less than" others, "slow," or "backward." Adults may view these young adults as underachievers. Perfectionists and underachievers have something in common—they compare themselves harshly to others. They see others as better than they are, and neither perfectionists nor underachievers are content with who they are. Both lack self-esteem.

How's Your Self-Esteem?

How's *your* self-esteem? Does Beth's story sound familiar? Do you sometimes feel awful inside, even though everything appears to be going fine on the outside? Do you wonder why you so often feel disappointed? Do you feel put down? Do you feel shy and embarrassed?

You can excel in many things but still feel bad or discouraged. When you have low self-esteem, you feel inadequate, as if you are missing something yet aren't quite sure what the missing piece is.

The following self-esteem quiz will give you insight about how healthy your self-esteem is and how it could be improved. Make a photocopy of the quiz or write your answers in a notebook. There are no wrong or right answers to these questions. You don't have to share the answers with anyone if you don't want to.

Self-Esteem Quiz

Answer the following questions with a score of:
3 if the statement is *always* true for you
2 if it is *sometimes* true for you
1 if it is *seldom* true for you
0 if it is *never* true for you

3...always true
2...sometimes true
1...seldom true
0...never true

_____ 1. I criticize myself. Even when others compliment me, I find something wrong with myself or the project I'm working on.

_____ 2. It is difficult for me to make a decision.

_____ 3. I focus on the negatives and forget the positives.

_____ 4. When I make a mistake, that is all I can think about. I forget about anything good that may have happened that day.

_____ 5. I feel different and awkward around others.

_____ 6. I don't like some parts of my body.

_____ 7. I feel frightened or very tense in new situations.

_____ 8. I pretend to be happy when I'm really unhappy or angry inside.

_____ 9. My parents or other adults put me down in one or many areas in my life.*

_____ 10. I've thought about killing myself.

_____ 11. Either one or both of my parents use alcohol or drugs, such as marijuana, wine, or beer.*

_____ 12. I don't try out for sports, drama, speech, or any extracurricular activity that will make me perform in front of others.

_____ 13. I am scared of what my future holds for me.

_____ 14. I either overeat or deprive myself of food.*

_____ 15. I use drugs or alcohol, such as beer, wine, marijuana, crack, or speed.

_____ 16. When I think others are wrong, I have a strong urge to correct them.

_____ 17. My parents' arguments usually involve threats of some kind.*

_____ 18. My parents are rigid and will not allow me to do things that other kids my age are able to do, such as attend a school dance.*

_____ 19. I have a family member who lives with me who is seriously emotionally disturbed or mentally ill.*

_____ 20. My parents do not set any rules for me; I can do as I please.*

_____ 21. I exaggerate or lie to get my point across.

_____ 22. I am afraid of what others might think of me if I tell them what I really feel or think.

_____ 23. It is very important for me to do things right.

_____ 24. I have been sexually or physically abused (refer to page 44 for a brief definition of sexual abuse).*

_____ 25. I have a disability that keeps me from being involved in activities other kids my age are involved in.

The asterisks (*) are explained on page 18.

Now, add up all your figures. The highest score you can receive is *75*. The closer you are to this number, the more important it is for you to build your self-esteem. In other words, the closer your score is to 75, the lower your self-esteem might be. You may find it comforting to know that low self-esteem is a common problem.

What Does My Score Mean?

If you scored between 45 and 75, building your self-esteem is one of the most important goals you can set for yourself right now. If you scored high on the test, you may be experiencing difficulties such as conflict with others, gossiping about others, plans that don't seem to turn out for you, or troubled friendships. Perhaps you use or abuse drugs or alcohol or are in a group of friends who use heavily. If you score in this range, seek the help of an adult who can give you guidance. Most importantly, care enough about yourself to start working on your self-esteem.

Most teens—and adults—score between 25 and 55. Scores in this range still indicate that it's important for you to work on improving your self-esteem. Take a close look at the statements where you scored the number 3. This is a specific area that you may need to work on.

Finally, if you gave yourself a 2 or 3 on any of the questions with the asterisk (*), chances are you come from a troubled family, in which problems exist that could directly affect your self-esteem. Chapter Four, on Troubled Families, will be especially helpful to you.

If you have discovered that you have low self-esteem, you are among the majority of teens—and adults. Although your self-esteem is something that is inside you, it was created by outside circumstances. The home you grew up in, advertisements, your financial situation, people's reaction to your disability, brothers and sisters, and others' expectations of you can all contribute to your self-esteem. Low self-esteem is something you *learned*. The good news is that now you can learn to have high self-esteem, to feel good about yourself.

CHAPTER TWO

Your Thoughts Can Hurt

How much of the day do you spend thinking negative thoughts? "I can't do that." "Everyone will think I'm weird." "My nose is too big." "I'm fat and ugly." "Nobody really likes me." "If I make a mistake, everyone will laugh at me." "I hate how this outfit looks on me." "What if she walks away when I start to talk to her?"

You may have seen the movie *Gremlins*. A teenage boy's father gave him a strange-looking pet and warned his son never to feed the creature after midnight. One night the boy lost track of time and fed the pet. The friendly, purring animal metamorphosed into a mean, destructive, dangerous Gremlin that could multiply by getting wet.

We all have a Gremlin inside us. When our Gremlins are "fed," it can mean trouble for us and those around us. But what are these Gremlins?

Gremlins are the many negative thoughts that we have about ourselves. We all have conversations in our heads about ourselves and the world around us all the time. One word for these thoughts is *self-talk*—an internal conversation. Gremlins, however, are the negative messages you tell yourself. Gremlins can stop you from speaking up, saying no to someone, taking risks, going on a field trip with students you don't know, or calling someone on the phone. These Gremlins are the *can'ts, shoulds, if onlys,* and *don'ts* you tell yourself. Gremlins stop you from feeling good about yourself.

Negative thoughts do multiply when we feed them. To win your battle against your Gremlins, you will need to learn what yours are and how they affect your life.

The "What If" Gremlin

Ryan recently encountered the What If Gremlin when he went to a school dance:

I went to the dance held before spring break. They had a disc jockey from the most popular radio station. When he played a slow dance, I would just stare and watch everyone else. I felt so stupid! I couldn't get near the girl I wanted to dance with. I'd see her standing there talking with other kids. I wanted to talk with her, but I'd think, 'What if she isn't interested in me? What if she says she doesn't want to dance with me in front of everyone?' So I waited for her to notice me and told myself that if she smiled at me I would go over and talk with her. She did smile at me, but then I wondered, 'What if she wasn't smiling at me?' I thought I'd wait until she smiled again and then I would...

Many people avoid taking risks because they're afraid of what *might* happen. What if the worst does happen? What if Ryan had been turned down in front of others? At worst, he would have felt embarrassed, but he also would have realized that he had the courage to ask someone to dance. He is guaranteed not to have the chance to dance with her if he doesn't take the risk and ask her. "What ifs" make the possible outcomes of your actions seem so frightening that you don't take the chance.

The "I'm Stupid" Gremlin

This Gremlin attacks our self-confidence through negative labels. Often when we consider taking a risk, a label such as "I'm stupid" or "I'm too lazy" interferes with our plans.

> Usually when I have an idea about something, I just keep it to myself. I figure that it is probably not that good of an idea or someone else would have come up with it. Of course, it's probably not such a bad idea and someone else in class usually does come up with it later. I just feel too embarrassed to share my ideas.
>
> —Avie, age 19

If Avie continues to keep her ideas to herself, she will feel bad that no one knows that she has some good ideas. Negative self-talk inhibits you from doing things you really want to do—such as telling others about your ideas. Other negative labels teens give themselves include: ugly, immature, dull, unladylike, bossy, selfish, wrong, wimp, sissy, jerk, geek, bitchy, crazy, pushy, weak, nerd, overreactive, self-centered, incapable, nosy, and overemotional.

"I was told I was bossy when I asked for what I wanted."
"I feel like a wimp because I didn't go out for football."
"If I wear this outfit I'll look like a geek!"

Life's Commentators

You've probably heard radio or television commentators describing sports competitions. Generally, they describe and "comment" on the event during and after the competition. They also predict what they believe will happen—who will win, who will lose. Once the winner has crossed the line or hit the last ball, the commentators have a lot to say about why someone won or lost.

The adults in your life—parents, teachers, relatives, neighbors—are your commentators. Brothers and sisters and peers can also be commentators. Your parents in particular probably comment quite a bit on you and your life. You learned most of your internal messages, negative or supportive, from what you heard adults tell you. Like sports announcers, the commentators in your life can be right on target sometimes. Maybe they told you that you might be too short to compete in basketball but said not to give up on other sports, and they were right—you didn't make the basketball team, but you were accepted for the swim team. At other times the commentators are wrong: they told you not to expect to do well in a writing contest, but you won. Listen carefully to what your commentators tell you. Just because they are adults does not mean that they are always right. Many adults say hurtful and negative things:

"Stop daydreaming your life away!"

"You can't do that. No one in our family is very good at that."

"You're a bad girl/boy."

"Don't do it unless you can do it right."

"That's just how things are around here."

"Shut up."

"Don't be so stupid."

"Shame on you."

"Why can't you be as good as your brother/sister?"

"It's your fault I feel this way."

"You're going to be the death of me and your father!"

"What's wrong with you, all the other students in the class understand the question."

"I think you can do better than that."

"Look at her, she's got bumps on her chest. She must be growing up."

"Be a man about it and forget it."

"Go out for basketball if you want to be popular."

Teasing is another way adults can make hurtful comments. Jokes and humor are great. But making fun of someone's body, behavior, disability, or ability is cruel.

We all deserve to have commentators who are supportive, who offer us advice, and who encourage us to take healthy risks. Most of us have at least one adult in our life who supports us.

Most negative comments could be said in a far more encouraging way. For example, "Stop daydreaming your life away," might be a poor way of saying: "Daydreaming is okay, but I want you to get some fresh air, too." This comment is supportive and offers some reasonable advice. Adults say hurtful comments either because they don't know how to communicate in a more positive way or because they are intentionally being cruel. If they are intentionally cruel, it is most likely because they have low self-esteem themselves. People with low self-esteem often take their bad feelings out on others.

You can't force the adults in your life to talk to you in a more supportive way. But you can take two important steps to defeat the negative commentators and improve your self-esteem. First, develop a relationship with an adult who is supportive and can give you helpful guidance. Second, try not to believe everything the negative commentators say. The truth is that you have a right to be *yourself*. You have the right to be different and experience life in your own way, at your own pace.

The "Don't" Gremlin

This Gremlin's big word is DON'T: "Don't get along with others." "Don't give that new guy a chance." "Don't be yourself." "Don't grow up." "Don't admit you have feelings." "Don't tell others what you want." "Don't take responsibility for your own life." "Don't take risks." These messages eat away at your self-esteem because they prevent you from just *being*. A common Don't Gremlin is "Don't be different."

You have the right to be different—to be you. Let's face it, high school is hard on anyone's self-esteem. It would be easier to not take on the responsibility of improving your self-esteem. Who wants to be different anyway? Isn't the goal to be like those you consider popular? But think about how you want your life to be as an adult.

These Gremlins obstruct creativity ("Don't take chances," "Don't be different"); success ("Don't take risks," "Don't take that college class, none of your friends are in it"); and happiness ("Don't be yourself"). They prevent you from taking responsibility for your life.

Many other negative beliefs or thoughts can inhibit our creativity and self-esteem. Here are some other examples of common negative beliefs:

Assuming the worst. "This will never work out." "It's going to rain all weekend and we'll have a lousy camping trip." "She hates me."

Blaming others for how you feel or behave. "It's his fault, he did it first!" "I wouldn't have done it if she hadn't asked me to."

Failing to see the whole picture—having tunnel vision. "She didn't like me, so none of her girlfriends will like me either." "I don't understand how smoking pot interferes with my studying."

Thinking in black-and-white terms. This means thinking that things are either this way or that way, with no room for in-between or a maybe. "It's never okay to be angry." "All girls care about is how they look." "All boys care about is themselves. I'll never trust them again."

Blowing things out of proportion—overestimating the importance of a situation or event. "This pimple on my face makes me ugly." "My disability makes me an unlikable person." "She didn't kiss me goodnight, which means she never wants to see me again. I must be a real jerk!"

All of us at one time or another believe these "faulty thoughts." Faulty thoughts are simply untrue. When we take a closer look at a situation, we may come to realize that we have the wrong idea about what's really happening. For example, Jeff walks into a room and hears someone say, "Oh, no!" He assumes that the "Oh, no" was about him and that no one in the room likes him. This is an example of faulty thinking—blowing things out of proportion and assuming the worst. In fact, the comment that Jeff heard was about something else, and there were actually quite a few people in the room who liked him.

The first way to get rid of these faulty thoughts is to recognize when you have them. Which ones are true for you? Now is a good time to work on getting rid of your Gremlins and faulty thoughts.

Ridding Yourself of Gremlins

As Eleanor Roosevelt said, no one can make you feel inferior without your consent. Even when the commentators in your life say negative things about you or your friends tease you, you can choose not to believe them.

To build your self-esteem, you must first eliminate your Gremlins. Think of them as taking up valuable space inside of you. Getting rid of them leaves room for something more positive. When you stop feeding your Gremlins, your good feelings will increase.

Try this exercise to help win the battle over your Gremlins. Draw a circle in the middle of a piece of paper. This circle represents you. Then, as shown on the next page, draw four lines coming from this inner circle to four other outer circles. These circles represent your Gremlins. The Gremlins can come from people, organizations, fictional characters, peers, or other commentators in your life. It's important to identify your Gremlins so you can begin to think about how they affect you.

These are Anne's Gremlins:

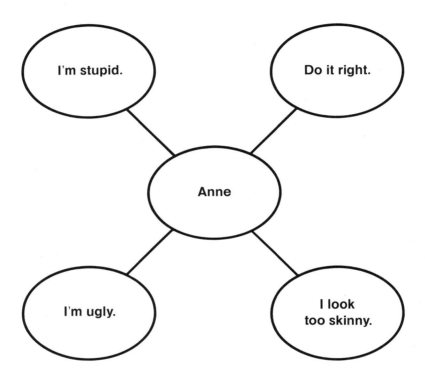

   The following exercise will also help you understand your Gremlins. Think about a recent event or situation in which you felt negative about yourself. First, describe the situation; then identify your negative thoughts or Gremlins; third, describe the feelings that accompanied this experience; and finally, write down what happened. Haley gives an example below of how she used this exercise to help her try out for the school play:

I wanted to try out for the last three plays but never got up the nerve to do it. My parents are always telling me how shy I am. I don't want to be shy, but the more they tell me I am, the more it seems to be true. After I found out what my Gremlins were saying to me, I decided to tell them to shut up! I began telling myself over and over that I have just as much chance to get a part as anyone. I want a part. Well, I got the part I wanted! Maybe now my parents will stop telling me I'm shy.

Situation	What I am telling myself (Your Gremlins)	Feelings	Result
Trying out for school play.	"I'm shy."	embarrassed	Didn't try out for play, didn't get a part.
	"I'll make a fool of myself."	scared	
	"This is a stupid idea."	stupid	
	"They've probably already chosen everyone ahead of time."	lonely	
		mad	

Think of a situation in your life when your Gremlins got in the way.

What we *think* has a big impact on what we *do* and consequently what happens to us. Because of this, the best way to begin building your self-esteem is by learning more supportive self-talk.

Chapter Three

Building Self-Esteem

It's a funny thing about life;
if you refuse to accept anything but the best,
you very often get it.
                                        —W. Somerset Maugham

There are many things locked up inside of me. It's almost like a song that keeps playing over and over deep inside of me. It's slow and steady most of the time. When I really listen to it, the song becomes a feeling. And this feeling tells me not to be afraid...to keep going...to be myself.
                                        —Caitlin, age 15

The first part of the book discussed the power of Gremlins and negative labels. This section is about the power that comes from using supportive self-talk. Since we all have a continuous conversation going on in our heads, a great step toward self-esteem is to make this conversation positive.

You can replace your Gremlins with *affirmations*. Affirmations are positive, supportive messages we say to ourselves. Supportive self-talk can make things happen for you. Just as the thought "I can't" may stop you from getting what you want, the belief "I can" will create possibilities for you. Every day you use your thoughts—your imagination—to create things. Gremlins create negative images, of failing, for example. Affirmations help you create health, enjoyable relationships, successful risks, attractiveness, and whatever else you may hope for.

> For the longest time I told myself I couldn't try out for speed skating. I was convinced I wasn't good enough. Any time I thought I might talk to the coach, a voice in my head said, 'Don't, you can't do that!' Finally I had an argument with myself. I asked, 'Well, why not?' This voice kept telling me the same things—all negative. But there was another voice that said, 'Go ahead and try it. You love to skate and you can be fast when you really want to be.' So I finally gave it a chance. I haven't won any races yet, but I'm on the team and it feels great! I know I can learn to do even better now that I've joined.
>
> —Paul, age 16

You may need to argue with yourself at times, too. The Gremlins will put up a strong fight, but if you don't feed them, they won't grow. Feed yourself with supportive talk instead. Supportive self-talk encourages you to take risks, comforts and reassures you, gives you hope and courage, and allows you to be different. Here are some examples of affirmations:

I can do it!

I am a lovable person.

I have a lot to offer.

I am beautiful/attractive/handsome.
I make a great friend.
I can learn anything I choose to.
The future holds good things for me.
I make smart and loving choices.
I am creative and proudly share my talents with others.
It's possible!
I take good care of myself.
I am growing into a healthy adult.
Something wonderful is going to happen today!

Remember the exercises on pages 28 and 29? You can now use these exercises to create supportive self-talk.

Draw four lines from the second set of circles (which represented the Gremlins in the exercise). Now you can add a third set of circles, which will represent your supportive talk.

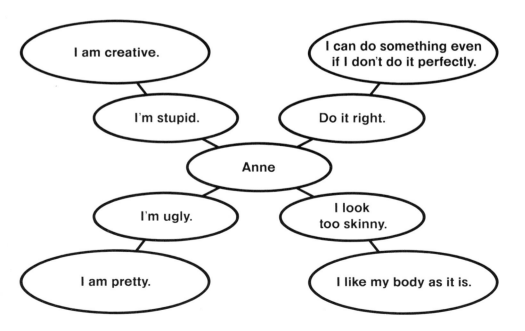

The second exercise can be used to help you take healthy risks, such as trying out for speed skating or asking someone out on a date. In the exercise below, Haley is giving herself supportive self-talk.

Situation	What I am telling myself (Supportive self-talk)	Feelings	Result
Trying out for school play.	"I can do it." "I want to be in the play." "This is a good idea." "I have a good chance to get a part."	excited nervous hopeful	Tried out for play, got a a part.

Think of your own situation to do the exercise using supportive talk.

Next time you find yourself stuck in negative thinking, ask yourself these questions:

1. What am I telling myself?

2. Is what I am telling myself helpful to me?

3. Do I recognize any Gremlins or negative labels here?

4. What supportive self-talk can I say to myself in this situation instead?

5. What action can I take that is helpful to me in this situation?

Supportive self-talk will have a positive impact on how you feel about yourself and on the choices you make. Affirmations encourage you to be unique and allow you to make mistakes. Self-talk gives you credit for the effort you put into something ("Good job!" "At least I tried."). Most importantly, supportive self-talk is guaranteed to build your self-esteem. At first it will probably feel strange to have this kind of conversation with yourself. As you practice talking to yourself in a supportive way, though, it will become more natural. You will find that you start talking nicely to yourself more and more. It's like learning a foreign language. It takes commitment and practice, but after a while, you will be fluent.

Supportive talk helps you create a new definition of yourself. Suppose you usually think of yourself as "not very smart, scared to talk to other people, and not very attractive." This can be the old definition of yourself. Now take the time to write out a *new* definition of who you are!

My old definition of me:

My new definition of me:

What about Hurt and Angry Feelings?

The teen years can be a mixture of great expectations and great disappointments. Because your body and life are changing, it's understandable that your emotions are also changing. The transition from childhood to adulthood brings a variety of intense emotions. You don't have to explain all your feelings to others; you may not even know why you feel the way you do at times. This is normal.

When adults around you are respectful of the changes you are going through, it's easier for you. But many times people do not understand the intensity of your feelings.

If I could tell adults, especially parents, one thing, it would be this: that we have *real* problems. So many adults treat me and my friends like what we're feeling isn't any big deal. How many times have I been told, 'It will pass,' or 'Give it time and it will go away.' When I was worried about school, my dad told me, 'Wait till you have to work every day, seven days a week.' I was real pissed at him. I also felt stupid, like my problems don't count.

—Kevin, age 17

Ever since my dad left I feel lousy. I've even thought of killing myself, even though I know I wouldn't do it. It's just that my mom hates my dad now, says he broke up the family. Anytime I do feel good, I end up feeling bad for my mom. I'm not sure what to do. It's all so lousy.

—Jason, age 15

Your feelings do count. It's important to pay attention to your feelings. Some teens harm themselves when they're feeling bad. They use drugs and alcohol, overeat or undereat, don't sleep, scar their bodies with knives or razors, isolate themselves from others, or take dangerous risks. These activities will only add to the hurt.

Instead, talk to others about your feelings. Try to express your feelings in a respectful way. The simplest way to do this is to tell someone else honestly how you feel: "I feel sad," "I feel angry about...," "I feel scared when...." Start by saying "I feel..." rather than "You make me feel...." Other people may behave in a way that brings up a feeling in you, but it is *your* emotion. Expressing feelings honestly means not blaming someone else for how you feel.

You may also want to write in your journal or write an "angry letter" to the person you are mad at. Keep the letter for yourself; it's not meant to be used as a way to hurt someone. Remember, all your feelings are okay. It is what you do with your feelings and how you express them that may be hurtful.

Self-Esteem Boosters

Self-esteem boosters are quick ways to help you feel better after a difficult day. When you feel down or disappointed, try one or more of these self-esteem boosters.

Talk to a friend, or anyone who supports and encourages you. Call a friend who can help cheer you up, or call your parent who no longer lives with you. Ask for some support and advice on what to do to feel better.

Make a list of the things you like and admire about yourself. List all your successes, what you like about your body, why you make a good friend, what you did this week that you are proud of, and so on....If you want, you can read the list out loud to yourself.

Give yourself some supportive talk. This is a good time to review your daily or weekly affirmations. Anytime you feel down or discouraged is a good time to say your supportive talk. Remember, feeling sad or discouraged is natural. You can feel sad and still remind yourself of good things to come.

Compliment someone. Let people know what you like about them. Make sure to choose someone who will accept your praise and attention. It feels good to compliment others, and they are more likely to let you know what they like about you, too. Everyone likes compliments!

Finish a project that you will feel great about completing.
This could be a school project or one you started for yourself at home. Remind yourself that there is really no such
thing as perfect. Give yourself lots of praise for finishing
the project.

***Try out for something that you know you have a very
good or sure chance of succeeding at.*** Remind yourself of
your skills or talents by trying out for a group or activity.
Try out for choir, if you are a good singer, or basketball if
you're athletic. You can decide later if you really want to
go through with it or not.

Take a short mini-vacation or adventure with friends,
family members, or alone. Spend a day at a park, museum,
or shopping mall, or visit someone you haven't seen for a
long time. Take a different bus route some Saturday and
have lunch in a restaurant that serves food from another
country. If you live in a small town or on a farm, consider
spending a day at a friend's house.

Cry, run, yell, or sing. Many times we simply need to allow
ourselves to *feel*, to express our feelings. If you are sad,
hurt, or disappointed, let yourself have a good cry. If you're
mad and want to yell, go ahead and yell. Yell out loud in a
place where you won't bother others. You could also turn
up the music and sing. Jamie has what she calls "mad
music." She turns up the volume on her compact disc
player and plays an "angry tune" while she dances and
sings in her room. You may want to do the same, or go for
a fast walk with your Walkman. Nathan finds it helpful to
work out at the gym.

Take a few minutes to read something uplifting. Read an
article in a magazine that's about feeling good. Or if you

have a book that is full of good news and adventure, read it. This is not the time to watch a lot of soap operas or read a murder story. Fill your mind with uplifting news.

Live up to an agreement you made with someone but haven't yet kept. Pay back a loan or part of a loan that is overdue. Call that friend or relative you said you would call. If you've been promising to help your parents with something, volunteer to help them.

Give up trying to be perfect. "Anything worth doing is worth doing poorly." Take responsibility for the effort you put into something. It's better to do something—even if it doesn't work out exactly the way you wanted it to—than to be stuck with unfinished projects and goals because you're worried that they won't be "perfect." Doing something in an average way is better than giving up completely.

As a Teenager You Have Rights

Did you know that as a teenager you have rights? If your rights are violated, you can get help in protecting them. This list is to be used as a guide to help you respect not only your own rights, but everyone's. If by following your goals you hurt others, then you are misusing your rights.

As a teenager you have the right:

▲ To have private thoughts. No one has the right to know all your thoughts.

▲ To not be physically or sexually abused. This right is protected by law.

▲ To be happy. You have the right to pursue your happiness as long as it doesn't jeopardize others' rights.

▲ To be safe. You have the right to live in a safe environment and neighborhood.

▲ To pursue your goals.

▲ To say no to anything that is against your best interest or safety.

▲ To try new and different things that promote learning and health.

▲ To choose how you feel about others (even when it is contrary to how adults feel).

▲ To hold a different opinion than others (this includes adults).

▲ To be proud of your inheritance. We all inherit looks, genes, culture, race, family, etc. You have the right to your inheritances and to be proud of them.

▲ To be treated respectfully by adults, friends, acquaintances, and strangers.

▲ To take your time and do things over if you need to. You have the right to do things as many times as necessary.

▲ To not do something perfectly and feel satisfied. Give yourself credit for the effort. When the result is not what you wanted, you can still feel satisfied because of the effort and risk you took in doing it.

▲ To be loved.

▲ To be given guidance and support when needed.

▲ To have a say in family decisions.

When you exercise your rights, you are saying to the world that you are an important person—that your feelings, beliefs, and desires count. One 14-year-old says, "My parents would freak out if I told them I was mad at them!"

Maybe this is true for you, too. You can, however, exercise these rights in a loving and respectful manner. One father tells how he appreciated his daughter telling him when she was upset:

> I'm proud that my 15-year-old daughter got mad at me for calling her by her nickname in front of her friends. She had already asked me not to call her this name in front of others, especially boys. But I forgot, and she later told me that she felt real embarrassed. I'm glad she trusted me enough to tell me.

CHAPTER FOUR

Troubled Families

No one starts out with low self-esteem. When we are born, we completely accept ourselves. But over time, our parents, teachers, brothers and sisters, friends, schoolmates, and boyfriends and girlfriends can chip away at our self-esteem. Girls may be brought up to believe that they have less creative potential than boys, for example. Their mothers were probably taught the same thing. Boys, on the other hand, are often taught to put physical strength ahead of everything else. Being "tough" is more important than having feelings.

If your parents lack self-esteem, chances are you lack it too. This does not make your parents bad people—it simply means that they could benefit from improving their self-esteem. Other problems within families can also undermine your self-esteem. This chapter discusses families that would be considered troubled. Some of these problems are much more serious than others. Incest is usually far more harmful than divorce, for instance. Divorce can actually be the best for everyone in the family, yet it still will affect your self-esteem. Refer to the resource list in the back of the book if you want more help with specific problems that exist within your family.

Alcoholism/drug abuse. Alcohol includes beer, wine, wine coolers, hard liquor, and various cough medicines. Drugs include marijuana (pot), hashish, cocaine, crack, speed, diet pills, valium, and acid, to name a few. Drugs and alcohol can be used in a *non*abusive way. For example, when prescribed by a physician, tranquilizers can be used for a short period of time to help someone through a rough time. However, use of any drug or alcohol can turn into abuse. Even drugs prescribed by a doctor can be abused. Generally speaking, abuse of a drug or alcohol is a misuse of it: using too much at one time; using it too often; using it at the wrong time; taking drugs that are dangerous; using prescribed drugs for something other than to heal from a sickness; depending on drugs to feel good. A family member's drug or alcohol abuse can affect your self-esteem. Also, you have a greater chance of abusing drugs and alcohol yourself if others in your family abuse.

If you think one (or both) of your parents abuses drugs or alcohol, talk about your concerns to another adult you trust. Perhaps together you can talk to your parents about your concern and about possible solutions, like getting the family to go to counseling. Most people don't stop alcohol or drug abuse without the help of either counselors or support groups. If your parents abuse alcohol or drugs, they need help, whether they admit it or not.

Divorce. When our parents no longer choose to be together, somehow we feel that this says something about us. Divorce also shakes us because we want to believe that when people make a serious commitment, they will stick to it. Life is constantly changing, however, and sometimes plans and commitments change too. If your parents don't get along and their divorce is bitter, it is hard on you. Parents who use their children to get even with each other are abusive—they are misusing their authority as parents. If this is true for you, try to remain as uninvolved in their conflict as possible, and seek help and support from outside the family. Many counselors who work with teens are from a divorced family themselves. Remember, parents divorce each other, not their children.

Death of a close family member. The death of a family member can cause great pain and confusion for the surviving family members. How the death is handled within your family will affect your self-esteem. The more open and honest people are about their feelings, the easier it will be for everyone to get through it. An unexpected death is difficult because you may not have had the chance to say goodbye to the person, or there may be something you wish you had had the chance to say. Death and loss are part of life. Death does not mean that this person had a special reason to die ("God liked her better or less"), or that you are being punished ("God took away someone I loved because I'm a bad person"). Sooner or later we all lose someone we love. If someone you love has died, talk to others about your feelings and about this person. The person may have died, but he or she remains very much alive within your heart and mind.

Emotional abuse. The definition of *abuse*, according to Webster's New World Dictionary, is "to hurt by treating badly; mistreat. To use insulting, coarse, or bad language about or to someone; to scold harshly." To abuse someone emotionally is to hurt her or him by saying mean things or acting mean. Emotional abuse includes hurtful teasing, neglect, putting someone down, name-calling, and swearing, screaming, or yelling at someone. Since we learn our self-talk from others, emotional abuse is harmful to our self-esteem.

Incest/sexual abuse. Incest is sexual contact between a child and an adult within the same family. Incest is against the law. Uncles, fathers, mothers, grandfathers, grandmothers, older brothers, and other relatives could commit incest. It can also occur between stepparents and their stepchildren. Sexual abuse can include any unwelcome touch by an adult. If you believe you or someone you know is being sexually abused, talk to another adult you trust. **It is not okay for anyone to touch you sexually if you don't want to be.**

Mental illness/serious emotional problems. A family member's mental illness or serious emotional problems can disrupt the whole family. When someone has a serious emotional problem or is mentally ill, his or her family is often in a continual state of crisis. Such continued stress is hard on everyone's self-esteem and well-being. There is help for you and your family. Refer to the back of the book for where to go for help.

Physical abuse. Physical abuse includes any form of hitting another person. Slapping, kicking, biting, shoving, and pushing are all forms of abuse. Any form of spanking that causes pain is abusive. A gentle spank that is intended to teach a child not to cross a busy street is not necessarily abusive. Most kids can be taught without being hit, however. The more the abuse is repeated, the more troubled the family. Physical abuse beats your self-esteem out of you. If you are in a physically abusive family, reach out for help. It is illegal for anyone to physically abuse you.

Neglectful families. Neglect includes parents and siblings who are indifferent—who don't seem to care much about what you do or don't do. Neglectful parents are not involved with you and your activities. They aren't available for emotional support and don't attend events that you participate in. In many families, one parent may be involved, while another remains uninvolved. You deserve to have friends and adults who care about you. If one or both of your parents is neglectful, invite other adults and friends to be involved with you.

What You Can Do

If you come from an abusive family, the best thing you can do is get help from someone outside the family. Go to a trusted adult: the school counselor, the youth director at the local community center, your rabbi or minister. Open up to them about what is happening in your home and ask for their support and guidance. It can be very difficult asking for help, because it might seem as if you are "telling" on someone in your family. But who do you help by keeping it a secret? If you or someone in your family is being abused, *everyone* needs help. The person who is abusing you also needs help. Most important, you deserve to be treated with love and kindness.

If you come from a troubled family, you face particular challenges and difficulties. It may help to know that many young people come from troubled families. You are not alone. One in four families has a member with mental illness; alcohol or drug abuse is a problem in at least six in ten families; divorce happens in about half of all families.

If you come from an abusive family, you can carry on the tradition of abuse or you can choose not to. You will help end the chain of abuse by building your own self-esteem. People with self-esteem—who feel good about themselves—do not abuse or mistreat others. Having self-esteem helps you confront problems, because you are strong inside.

CHAPTER FIVE

Differences

We all want to feel that we belong. It helps if we belong to a healthy family. But there is another "family" of which we are all a part. This is the family of *people*. This family includes everyone from every race, nation, and background. We all have many things in common. Most importantly, we share our larger "home" of the Earth. Unfortunately, for some people, "different" means "bad."

The difference may be skin color, a disability, religion, sexual orientation, a way of speaking, or political beliefs. Sometimes people put others down in order to feel more powerful or better about themselves. The word *prejudice* refers to a dislike of someone because of the person's difference. We often learn our prejudices from the adults in our life. To belong to the larger family of people, we must fight the prejudices within ourselves and those that exist in our community. It is up to you whether or not you want to exclude people because they have a different color of skin or hold different beliefs than you. But if you do exclude someone, you'll miss out on what could be a great relationship.

Jerome looks different from everyone. He says it is because he has Black, Indian, and Hmong in him. He's a great soccer player. We play on the same team at school. I've been wanting to invite him along with me and my friends, but I don't think my friends like Jerome. One called him a 'geek' and a 'nigger.' I was pissed but I didn't say anything. I guess my friends aren't that great if they call Jerome names. They just don't know him like I do. He's a better soccer player than anyone and he's cool too. Come to think of it, I think I like Jerome better.

—Mike, age 18

Mike doesn't have to choose between his friends and Jerome if he doesn't want to. But Mike's friends may decide not to hang out with him if he invites Jerome along. That's too bad for them, because they will miss out on all that Jerome *and* Mike have to offer. Prejudice interferes with friendships. A prejudiced person has low self-esteem and tries to build himself up by putting others down. For a while, putting someone down may make this person feel superior, but it won't last.

My mother gave me the best advice about why I shouldn't go along when others are putting someone down. She asked me once, 'What do you think they say about you when you aren't around?' This made me think. They probably talk badly about me too. I decided to let others know that I do not want to hear or talk badly about others. When I can't speak up, I just walk away.

—Jeannie, age 16

You can continue a friendship with someone whom you believe has prejudices. You don't have to agree with your friends about everything. This does not mean you should pretend that it is okay to put someone else down, however. Speak up and let others know what you think and how you feel. You will find that many other kids and adults are willing to learn and change. Give others a chance instead of giving up. With your increased self-esteem, you can accept them, differences and all.

Body Image

My body makes me sick. My legs are long and look like poles; I have no breasts and my hair is too thin to do anything with. My mom keeps telling me that I look fine and everything will fill out in time. I wish I could stay home until I grew breasts and my hair got thicker!

—Debbie, age 16

I read in a fashion magazine that shoulder-length hair is outdated. And there I was with hair hanging around my shoulders. I've been trying to grow it out forever, but I went and cut it and now I really hate it! Then I began to wonder what else I would change if a magazine article told me it was outdated?

—Kristen, age 17

Just how much is my body going to change? Because I
can't stand it the way it is now.

—Kurt, age 15

Teens often feel uncomfortable with their bodies because
they are changing so much. If you're like most teens, you
are probably dissatisfied with some part of your body. Try to
be kind to yourself—there are many kinds of body shapes
and sizes. No two bodies are exactly alike.

If you have a group of friends, the group probably has
ideas about what looks right for a boy or a girl. You may feel
pressured to look a certain way yourself. The pressure to be
in style is tremendous for teens. Advertisements, magazines,
family, and friends influence how you feel about your body
and appearance, and their opinions often affect your choice
of clothing and hairstyle. It probably seems difficult to just
be yourself. Advertisements teach us that girls should be
thin, pretty, and feminine and that guys should be tall,
muscular, and hairy. Parents may also have strong opinions
about how you should look. Sometimes they are being pro-
tective of you, while other times they have reasons that
they might not be aware of. For example, if your dad was
overweight as a teen, he might try to control your diet.

Teachers and other adults may unintentionally make rude
or condescending comments about your body changes.

I have a lot of hair all over my body. My homeroom teacher
last year would teasingly call me 'ape.' It was humiliating,
especially if any of the girls in the room overheard!

—Chad, age 17

Maybe one reason the homeroom teacher was rude was that he was uncomfortable with his own body. It's best for Chad not to take what the teacher says personally. He may also want to approach the teacher after class and let him know that the teasing embarrasses him. If this doesn't work, Chad may want to ask his parents to talk to this teacher.

It's your body. And it will be changing throughout your teen years. In fact, our bodies continue to change until we die. Try to treat your body as if it were your best friend. Focus on what you like about your body and face, rather than criticizing what you wish were different.

Your body is okay just as it is. Try to let go of all the pressure from others to look a certain way. Try to create your own look. Wait three days before making any drastic physical changes, such as piercing your nose, dyeing your hair, or getting a tattoo. This will give you time to think about whether this change is really right for you. Remember that advertisers are selling their products. They want you to believe that you have to buy their advertised products in order to feel better about yourself. All advertisements exaggerate the effects of their products. If you look closely at others, you will see that we are all different shapes and sizes. It is only in magazines and movies and on television that people look "perfect."

The Real Body Shop

Try this exercise. Look at yourself in the mirror. Notice all that you *do* like about your body and face. Compliment yourself. Don't judge by what others say to you or compare yourself to advertisements or magazine photos. Think of ways you can enhance the parts of your body you like. If you really like how your hair looks, show it off. If you think your arms look strong, wear a sleeveless shirt when the weather allows.

Accept that:
- ▲ you're growing and changing at a fairly quick pace;
- ▲ your disability, if you have one, need not take away from all your physical abilities;
- ▲ your uniqueness makes you special, not weird.

Treat your body well by exercising and eating healthy foods. You are growing into a beautiful adult.

But I Have a Disability!

Can people who are deaf, mentally ill, or retarded feel good about themselves? Does having muscular dystrophy, a learning disability, or a disfigured face or body mean you can't have self-esteem? How can a disabled person—maybe you or someone you know—feel proud or happy?

A disability does not exclude you from having self-esteem. Everything in this book will work for you if you are disabled. Disabilities make you *different,* not bad. Being deaf makes you different, but it does not make you stupid, weird, or untalented. Many people would even disagree that their disability makes them "handicapped." The words handicapped and disabled imply that the person is less able than someone who isn't disabled.

Why is my deafness considered a disability? I can do anything you can do. Yes, I can even *hear*! It's just that I 'hear' with my eyes rather than my ears.

—Brian, age 19

The more self-esteem we have, the more we are able to accept our own and others' differences. If you have what society considers a disability, here are some additional ideas about how to build your self-esteem:

▲ Remember that everyone is different. You have many traits that make you different; your disability is just one.

▲ Focus on your abilities. Don't let your disability get in the way of showing what you know and can do.

▲ Accept your differences. Accept that your disability may make certain activities more difficult for you. Be patient with yourself and others.

▲ Reach out to other teens. Make friends with others who have disabilities. But don't limit yourself to only deaf friends if you are deaf, for example.

▲ Help change the world! Don't give up on others who are ignorant about your disability. Try to teach others about you and your differences. There will be people who can see beyond the difference and discover that the difference makes you special.

▲ Get involved in social activities that others your age are involved in, regardless of the challenge it presents to you. You have the right to experience all kinds of activities—dances, outings, projects, whatever. Don't exclude yourself.

▲ Be kind to yourself, and allow yourself and others to make mistakes when it comes to responding to your disability.

Chapter Six

Making Choices

For a teen, every day is filled with choices. Some are quite difficult, while others seem to come more easily. To make some decisions, you will need guidance and support from the adults in your life. You can make other decisions with the help of friends or on your own.

Difficult Decisions

You are going to be trying a lot of new things as a teen. Sometimes your decisions will seem simple and you will succeed. Other times, your decisions will result in failure. That's how it is for everyone. It can be hard to hold on to your self-esteem during the difficult times. If you don't get the encouragement you deserve from your parents, it is a good idea to talk to another adult, such as a relative, a staff person at your local community center, a youth leader at your church or synagogue, a teacher, or a school counselor.

Your parents or others may advise you not to smoke marijuana, not to shop downtown, not to hang around with a certain group of kids, not to drink, not to lie, or not to have sex before you are an adult. When it comes right down to it, though, it is *you* who will decide whether or not to follow their advice. You're the one who will decide what you will and will not do.

You're the one who decides whether to risk getting caught if you decide to go downtown against your parents' advice. It is you who will be with friends who want to smoke marijuana, and it is you who will risk being teased if you refuse. And it will be you who wonders whether you want to go further sexually with the person you have been dating for three months. You are the one who has to live with the decisions you make.

Many times the decision that is best for you—the one that you feel is right—can be the most difficult to make. It's not easy to say no to your friends, for example. It may be difficult to choose between going shopping with friends or doing your homework. It can be hard to decide not to go any further sexually, because you are afraid of the response you will get.

A Fairy Tale

Long, long ago, a boy was wandering in the woods at dusk on his way back from what should have been a successful hunt. But the boy hadn't caught a grouse, or even a squirrel, after a full day in the woods. He was ashamed. He could not decide whether to stay out through the cold night in the hope of catching an animal in the morning or to return home empty-handed, humiliated and embarrassed. While he was thinking about this, he realized it was getting very dark. He wasn't quite sure where he was anymore. He feared he might have wandered into the enchanted corner of the forest, where wizards, ghouls, fairies, and other magical creatures lived. And before long, indeed, a wizard, quite large and dressed in blue and silver, appeared before him. The boy was glad to see it was a wizard. Wizards were known to like children. "Can you help me find my way out of the woods?" the boy asked.

"Yes," said the wizard, "but you must tell me whether you want to go home or stay out all night so you can hunt again."

The boy couldn't decide. He wanted to go home, but he was embarrassed and afraid that the other boys would laugh at him. "I can't decide," the boy whispered to the wizard.

"Very well," said the wizard, sympathetically. He then placed in front of the boy two frogs. One frog was quite a bit larger than the other. The wizard told the boy, "If you want to get out of the woods, you must eat both frogs."

The boy, who was smart, didn't argue with the wizard, although he felt a little sick at the thought of eating two ugly frogs. The boy stood silent for a moment, thinking about his situation. The more he thought about it, the bigger and uglier the larger frog became.

"Can you help me with this?" the boy asked the wizard, as the large frog continued to grow.

"Yes. I will give you the best advice I can. You must eat both frogs to get out of the woods. So eat the larger one first and do it now." And with that the wizard disappeared.

The boy ate the big frog immediately, without thinking about it a moment longer. The remaining frog was so small in comparison that swallowing it was very easy. As he swallowed the little frog, the boy found himself standing only a few feet from the door of his home. He went inside. His family greeted him warmly, and although his brothers did tease him a bit, the boy was too glad to be home to really care.

Sometimes good advice is hard to swallow. Occasionally we have to decide between two difficult choices—like staying out in the cold woods or returning home and getting teased. Sometimes losing friends or being teased is better than doing something that may harm you, like trying a drug.

You can learn to walk away from people who want you to do something you don't want to do. Begin looking for friends who like the same things you do and who won't put you down or tease you if you make choices that are different from theirs. Most likely, the people who don't want you to make your own choices aren't very good friends anyway.

Making Your Own Choices

Try eating the biggest frog first—making the toughest choice or doing the more difficult task—for one week. Each day, decide what your biggest frog is and do that first. Whether it means getting your work out of the way or taking a difficult stand with friends, swallow the big frog first. It could be as simple a decision as choosing to do the most unpleasant errand first, or a more difficult choice, like deciding to tell your boyfriend you won't be going any further sexually.

I didn't want to go out with her anymore, but I couldn't decide how to tell her. I thought about writing her a note, calling her on the phone, or just avoiding her. I suppose the nicest thing to do would be to talk to her, but I was afraid she would start crying or something. The longer I waited to tell her, the harder it became. Finally, I wimped out and just avoided her. This is a big hassle, since our lockers are real close to each other. Why didn't I just tell her!

—Richard, age 17

Richard's big frog was to be honest with the girl he had been dating for six months. When you realize that it is important for you to make a decision, it may help to take these steps to make it simpler.

Decision-Making Steps
1. Stop and relax—give yourself time to make the decision.
2. Name the problem or challenge.
3. Make a list of your choices or possibilities.
4. Write out or clearly describe what the result/consequences will be of each choice.
5. Decide—make your choice.
6. Do it now.

Here's an example. Jody has been asked out on a date by a very popular guy, Perry. Perry is well liked by everyone, and Jody's friends would do anything to go out with him. But Jody's been told that Perry expects his dates to do more than just kiss, and two of her friends have gotten drunk on a date with him. Jody likes Perry, but she doesn't want to drink. She doesn't want to feel pressured to kiss him on the first date. To make her situation more difficult, her parents found a babysitting job for her the night of her date. She'd been asking them to help her find ways to earn some extra money. She has to decide before the weekend and feels rushed to tell Perry and her parents her plans. Here are Jody's decision-making steps:

1. Jody relaxes and tells Perry that she will let him know tomorrow whether or not she wants to go out with him on Friday. It was difficult to put him off, but she's glad she did.

2. She writes down a description of the problem: "I have to choose between going out with Perry and babysitting. I also have to choose whether or not I really want to go out with Perry."

3. Jody writes her options:

* Tell Perry I already made a commitment to babysit and let him know I would like to go out another time. Then go to my babysitting job.

* Tell Perry I'm babysitting that night and not show any interest in him. Then go to my babysitting job.

* Tell Perry that I am uncomfortable going out with him and would like to have him over to my house first. Then I tell my parents that I'll take the babysitting job.

* I cancel on both Perry and babysitting and go to a movie with friends.

4. Jody writes out the consequences of each choice:

* I get the babysitting job and the possibility of going out with Perry some other time, although he may change his mind about me.

* I'll babysit but lose the chance to go out with Perry if I'm rude to him.

* Perry may think I'm stupid or childish because I don't want to kiss or drink. Again, I'll have the babysitting job.

* I'll miss out on both the date and the job and will probably feel guilty if I go to a movie. My parents may not help me get another job.

5. Jody's decision is to tell Perry she got a babysitting job and let him know that she's interested in going out with him some other time. She's also giving herself time to decide if she really wants to go out with him.

6. She decides to call Perry after dinner. She'll tell her parents that she will take the job.

Accept Your Mistakes and Move On

Being a teen means experimenting with many new ideas and people. It's a time when you'll probably make mistakes. Sometimes you will try things that you'll decide aren't for you. When you make a choice, accept that it may result in a mistake. Mistakes are part of life—part of being human. Try not to be too hard on yourself when you make a mistake. No one is perfect. All you can do is your best, and if you are wrong, be willing to say you're sorry. Making a bad decision does not make you a bad person. It just means you goofed up, like we all do at times.

Most of the time I want others to treat me like an adult. I want to decide for myself about what to do. But other times I think, Hey, I'm still a kid! I don't want to have to pretend I don't need help.

—Tony, age 15

CHAPTER SEVEN

A Greater Power

*God's gift to you is your life—what
you do with your life is your gift to God.*
                                        —unknown

There are days when I really need God. I'm not so sure
God hears me, but I keep talking and hope that he's listening. I sure hope prayers are answered.

                                        —Rebecca, age 16

When I'm happy, God seems to disappear. When I'm
pissed, he shows up again, and we have a talk.

                                        —Kevin, age 17

I want so much to find God. But where is God? Everyone I
talk to has a different idea. I wish God sent letters. My letter
would tell me that everything is going to turn out all right
and how to get my dad to stop drinking. It would say the
reason my dad drinks isn't because he doesn't love us.

                                        —Marnie, age 14

As a teen, you feel many yearnings: sexual, mental, physical, social, and spiritual. As one 16-year-old said, "There's a fire inside of me. Sometimes it burns hard and hot and I have to do something about it. Other times it is softer, but it is always burning." The teen years are perhaps the most intense, filled with questions and changes. It is an important time of mental, physical, and spiritual growth. "Spiritual" refers to your relationship with God as you understand him or her. It involves the part of you that yearns for an explanation of life and for a sense of peace and belonging.

It would help to have proof that there is a power greater than all the troubles and challenges you face. That's what faith is about—believing that there is a greater power, without proof. Faith is trusting that good can come from troubled times, that you are not alone, that God or a greater power is listening and cares about what happens to you and your loved ones. Faith is having hope—and hope can be a very powerful form of support, especially during difficult times.

God can be understood in many ways and has many names. God is known to different people in different forms: a powerful force in the universe, Allah, the Almighty, the Great Spirit, the Creator, the Father, nature, divine spirit, and Supreme Being, to name a few. Every society has a name for God. Generally, God represents a power greater than humans. This power can help restore peace and happiness.

It may be easier for you to understand God as someone you are in a relationship with, rather than as an invisible force that will take away all your problems. Your part in the relationship is to develop into a healthy adult and to love and respect yourself and others. God's part is to be there as you struggle and grow.

It's common to blame God for all that has gone wrong in our lives. We may wonder where God is when we need him or her. Most of the problems in the world can be traced to human mistakes and cruelty, however. Problems occur when we misuse the power we have. It's up to you to live up to your half of the relationship.

When we let God help us, somehow we feel stronger and more capable. When events don't turn out as we had hoped, God can help us pull through. It can help to pray when you feel sad—or happy. While prayer is like asking for help from God, meditation is like listening to God's response. Meditation is simple—it's taking a few minutes in your day to be alone and sit quietly. Meditation is a time to gently repeat your affirmations and other supportive self-talk. One affirmation that can be used during meditation to help you listen to your inner voice is, "Be still and know that I am God." This allows you to tune into the quietness that is within you. God is often understood as a gentle, caring voice within us.

A Simple Meditation

Try this exercise once a day for one week. Sometime during the day or evening, find a private place where you will be undisturbed for five minutes. Sit in a chair in a comfortable position with both feet on the ground. Let yourself relax, then close your eyes. Bring to mind a prayer you have for your greater power. It can be anything, like asking for help with a test or a way to handle a problem. After you have told God your prayer, relax more by listening to your breathing. Notice how your chest rises as you inhale and falls as you exhale. Focus your attention on your breathing. Then choose one of your affirmations and repeat it slowly to yourself five times. In between each repetition, sit quietly and listen. Do any helpful thoughts come to you? Do you feel a little more peaceful about your problem? After you have repeated your affirmations, continue to sit breathing quietly. When you feel ready, slowly open your eyes. Look around the room and take a deep breath. If you want, write in your journal any thoughts or experiences you had during your meditation.

EPILOGUE
You Make a Difference

*How can I accept a limited definable self
when I feel, in me, all possibilities?*
—Anaïs Nin

I remember my teen years as filled with difficulties, with some fun and quiet times in between. I had trouble "fitting in" and couldn't find a place for myself. I had athletic ability, but I thought of athletes as "jocks" who didn't care about much besides athletics, so I chose not to try out for any sport. I was intelligent, yet I had a hard time getting along with teachers. Soon I was skipping classes. Luckily, I was chosen to attend an alternative free school, where I finished my last two years of high school. I began to enjoy learning and decided to go on to college—not sure at the time what I wanted to study.

All through my teens, I loved to write and I filled many notebooks with my thoughts and poems. I also spent hours volunteering at community organizations, because I loved working with people. Yet when I entered college I lacked many of the academic basics and had to start from scratch. Many adults discouraged me from thinking of myself as a writer. I was told I couldn't spell and had much to learn. I was warned that writing was a competitive field in which very few succeed. I was also cautioned not to enter the social work field since there were few jobs and little income.

To further my challenges, my father was gone most of the time, working to provide for the family. Although I benefited from his ability to financially support us, his presence and influence was missed in my life and in those of my brothers and sisters. When I turned 13, one of my brothers was diagnosed with schizophrenia, a serious mental illness. This disrupted his life and the lives of each of us in the family. As a result, we experienced a lot of pain and crisis for many years.

But some powerful factors in my life overrode the negativity and difficulty. These factors were a belief in myself, a strong relationship with my greater power (although there were times when I wondered where God was!), and some adults and friends who believed in me.

Some power within me told me that I deserved to feel good, I deserved to succeed, and that I could make good things happen in my life. My friends always supported me when I talked about my dreams and hopes of writing and of helping others. And I believed in their dreams as well. My mother encouraged me to take risks, to not let others' harsh opinions influence me, and, most importantly, to believe in myself. I can recall the names and faces of the few teachers who touched my mind and heart, encouraging me to use my energy and talent in healthy ways. Each of these people strengthened the power within me.

You too have this power inside you. Regardless of your outside circumstances, you deserve to feel good about your life, and you can make a positive difference in the world.

Everyone has a valuable gift or talent to share with the world. It may be complicated or quite simple. It could be an art or a science. It could be a sport or an ability to help others. Your talent may be as a loving parent or as a creative teacher. There are as many possibilities as there are people! As you build your self-esteem and become more and more yourself, this gift will come forth. It will be something you love to do and something that is fairly easy for you. By building your self-esteem, you will move beyond your teen years into an adult life that is full of experiences to CELEBRATE!

Resources

Troubled Families, Abuse, and Addictions

Alcoholics Anonymous (AA)
Box 459, Grand Central Station
New York, NY 10163

AA is a national network of groups and resources for alcoholics and their families. To find a local group, you can look in the white pages of your telephone book under AA or Alcoholics Anonymous.

Al-Anon Family Groups/Alateen
1372 Broadway
New York, NY 10106

Al-Anon is a fellowship of people whose lives are affected by alcoholism in a family member or close friend. There's probably a group near you.

Childhelp USA
6463 Independence Avenue
Woodland Hills, CA 91367
818-347-7280

Childhelp is a national group that combats child abuse— physical, emotional, and sexual— through treatment, prevention, and research. If you are not sure whether the problem you're experiencing is abuse, you can write or call Childhelp for information that may help you decide.

Cocaine Abuse Hotline
1-800-COCAINE

You can call this number any time of day or night with questions or concerns. They will refer you to a local group.

Family Service America
11700 West Lake Park Drive
Park Place
Milwaukee, WI 53224
1-800-221-2681

Family Service America is a network of several hundred agencies that provide family counseling. Call for a referral to an agency in your town.

National Clearinghouse for Alcohol and Drug Information
P.O. Box 2345
Rockville, MD 20852
This is a government agency that provides information about all types of drugs, alcohol, and addictive diseases.

PRIDE Drug Info Hotline
1-800-241-7946
This hotline provides taped information on a variety of topics related to drug and alcohol abuse, including resources for treatment. The line is available from 5:00 P.M. to 8:30 A.M. (EST) on weeknights and all day on weekends.

Disabilities

National Easter Seal Society
70 East Lake Street
Chicago, IL 60601
Assistance and information about services for people with disabilities.

National Information Center for Handicapped Children and Youth
P.O. Box 1492
Washington, D.C. 20013
Information and referrals to resources for young people with disabilities.

Body Image, Health, Sexuality

Overeaters Anonymous (OA)
P.O. Box 92870
Los Angeles, CA 90009
OA has local chapters nationwide with groups for youth and adults who have a problem with overeating or other eating disorders.

Society for Adolescent Medicine
19401 East U.S. Highway 40
Suite 120
Independence, MO 64055

For a list of teen clinics, physicians, and other health care professionals in your area, send a self-addressed, stamped envelope to the address above.

Teen Rights

National Association of Counsel for Children
1205 Oneida Street
Denver, CO 80220

A network of professionals concerned with the legal rights and protection of young people. Also provides information about juvenile law.

Emotional Health and Self-Esteem

Adolescent Hotline (National Runaway Switchboard)
1-800-621-4000

You can call this toll-free hotline 24 hours a day and talk to someone about your problems, whether you feel in imminent danger of suicide or not.

Emotions Anonymous/Youth Emotions
    Anonymous
P.O. Box 4245
St. Paul, MN 55104

Emotions Anonymous offers groups for youths to gain better emotional health.

LEAP Program for Teens
(Learning Effective Assertiveness and Power)
P.O. Box 19067
Minneapolis, MN 55419

LEAP offers in-services, groups, and materials for schools and other organizations interested in starting LEAP/self-esteem groups for teens and young adults.

For Further Reading

Bell, Ruth, et al. *Changing Bodies, Changing Lives: A Book for Teens on Sex and Relationships.* New York: Random House, 1988.

Burns, David. *Feeling Good: The New Mood Therapy.* New York: William Morrow & Co., 1980.

Coombs, H. Samm. *Teenage Survival Manual.* Lagunitas, CA: Discovery Books, 1989.

Day by Day: Meditations for Young Adults. Hazelden Meditation Series. San Francisco: Harper/Hazelden, 1988.

Fields, Rick, et al. *Chop Wood, Carry Water: A Guide to Finding Spiritual Fulfillment in Everyday Life.* New York: St. Martin's Press, 1984.

Rosenberg, Ellen. *Growing Up Feeling Good: A Growing Up Handbook Especially for Kids.* New York: Penguin Books, 1989.

Zerafa, Judy. *Go For It.* New York: Workman Publishing, 1982.

INDEX

Other helpful books from Lerner's Coping with Modern Issues series:

Coping with Death and Grief
by Marge Eaton Heegaard

Eating Disorders
A Question and Answer Book about Anorexia Nervosa and Bulimia Nervosa
by Ellen Erlanger

Family Violence
How to Recognize and Survive It
by Janice E. Rench

Feeling Safe, Feeling Strong
How to Avoid Sexual Abuse and What to Do If It Happens to You
by Susan Neiburg Terkel and Janice E. Rench

Teen Pregnancy
by Sonia Bowe-Gutman

Teen Sexuality
Decisions and Choices
by Janice E. Rench

Teen Suicide
A Book for Friends, Family, and Classmates
by Janet Kolehmainen and Sandra Handwerk

Understanding AIDS
by Ethan A. Lerner, M.D., Ph.D.

Understanding Mental Illness
For Teens Who Care about Someone with Mental Illness
by Julie Tallard Johnson

Understanding Sexual Identity
For Gay and Lesbian Teens and Their Friends
by Janice E. Rench